A Scent of Lilac
and other poems

These poems have been previously published in Northern Lakes' *Soundings, What's Playing?* and *The Hometown Gazette.*

A Scent of Lilac
and other poems

by LaMoine MacLaughlin

Northern Lakes Press
Northern Lakes Center for the Arts, Inc.

Published in 2009 in the United States of America by
  The Northern Lakes Press
  Northern Lakes Center for the Arts, Inc.
  113 Elm Street
  Amery, Wisconsin 54001

© Copyright 2009 by LaMoine MacLaughlin

All rights reserved. No part of this publication may be reproduced or transmitted in any form or by any means, electronic or mechanical, including photocopy, recording, or any information storage and retrieval system, without permission in writing from the author.

ISBN 978-0-9825194-0-0

Printed and bound in the United States of America
Library of Congress Control Number: 2009907001

This book is dedicated to
my wife, Mary Ellen,
and to all of my family and friends.

My Muse

She danced upon the sparkling air
    As twilight settled into night,
Then touched my eyes, implanting there
    Her gift of sight.

She scooped my heart clean to its core,
    Placed all past contents out of reach,
And crammed it full of verbal store:
    Her gift of speech.

She let her hair swirl in the wind,
    The raucous flight of screaming birds,
And then upon my lips she pinned
    Her gift of words.

She softly whispered through the trees
    A tune (I tried to hum along),
And, smiling, sent me on that breeze
    Her gift of song.

She sat beside me silently
    To watch one final, floating leaf,
Then quietly she shared with me
    Her gift of grief.

Lake Magnor Ice

Like Magnor Lake our age and its debris
    Lie firmly iced, and February wind
    Deafens numbed ears and leaves eyes nearly blind
To innuendo and to subtlety.

In March, what frigid phoenix dreams of flight,
    Of frolicking with wind on liquid wings?
    Within these hollow depths what soft muse sings
To make our hearing whole and heal our sight?

April, release Lake Magnor's shores so long
    Encased in cold, force life through frozen earth
    And loosen lulling waves in a rebirth
Of poetry, a renaissance of song.

Daedalus

These feathered words form not my wings
    Nor billow me from ground,
Though high aloft my spirit sings
    In ecstasy unbound.

Breath carries quintessential flight:
    Would words and I were one
With wind among these clouds of white
    Ascending toward the sun.

A Scent of Lilac

Part One: The Promise

Warm April rains rinse winter's hillsides clean,
Restoring icy fields to fertile green,
And geese fly north from southern wintering,
Beckoned by silent summonings of spring.
One April Petra Symonowski learned
That what she thought the flu and twinged and churned
Within her belly represented twins
(She always thought them penalties for sins),
A pair of twins to be September born
Amid the tasseling of summer corn.

All during May and June her waist grew thick
And Petra, so monotonously sick,
Saw shadows everywhere; a somber breeze
Sang mockingly among her peonies.
In time Petra ballooned beyond her dress
And plummeted into a dark distress;
She whispered to her husband in July
That she had dreamed she was about to die,
So Petra prayed, "O Heart of Jesus, scour
My soul of sin; save me in this dark hour!"

Then privately she swore a binding oath
That if their lives were spared, her babies both
Would walk that road in service to the Lord;
To all of this she pledged her sacred word.
And when their birthing time at last arrived,
She wondered later how they all survived.
Beneath the pushing and the tearing pain,
She vowed to never go through this again,
But when the pushing and the pain were done,
She held a daughter and she held a son.

The boy was baptized Martin for the way
He fought to finally see light of day;
The girl was baptized Marta. So these two,
Martin and Marta Symonowski, grew
Up strong and healthy on a little farm
Among green hills which sheltered them from harm.
Alone upon the porch Marta would swing
And listen to far-off cicadas sing;
As breezes moved among the spruce tops there,
A scent of lilac filled the evening air.

One special Sunday Petra wept for joy
To see her solemn son an altar-boy.
Soon little Martin started playing Mass,
Lifting the bread and chalice-drinking glass,
Pronouncing mumbled Latin mimicked well,
With Marta altar-boy to ring the bell.
And all who saw him doubted not the least
That one day Martin would become a priest,
A pastor surely, maybe even more,
Perhaps a stately, red-robed monsignor.

Slowly the chain of life linked year to year
Until Martin announced for all to hear,
"I want to be a priest!" and Petra smiled,
Remembering the promise for her child.
The news of Martin seminary bound
Confirmed what many felt for miles around,
Though how word traveled in that idle age
Was anybody's guess and no one's gauge.
Tears flowed like rivers on his leaving day
And Marta, waving, watched him drive away.

Life in this small Wisconsin valley place
Tried to resume its easygoing pace
But chores backed up and Father realized
His little farm was far too over-sized
For one man's work. He hoped an able hand
Would turn up soon, for jobs were in demand
During those thirties' lean depression days,
Especially once winter's icy glaze
Made tricky tramping it from farm to farm
For coffee, bread, and lodging dry and warm.

So when he stopped and asked, "Does anything
Around here need repair? Or could I bring
In wood? Sam Adams Holland is my name –"
They didn't really care from where he came.
Father offered, "Good food, a roof and bed
Are all we have." "A place to lay my head
At night and some hot soup are all I need,"
Sam Holland answered. "Come on, then, let's feed
The stock," Father replied. And Sam worked hard,
Earning respect and everyone's regard.

Those autumn days flew into winter weeks
And soon spring months sent torpid ice-bound creeks
Bubbling beyond their banks. Although he tried
To mind his work, Sam Holland could not hide
The times he stood befuddled and spell-bound,
Especially when Marta came around.
And Petra sensed a change in Marta too,
Whose daydreams nearly vanished her from view,
Transporting her to some far fairy-land,
Especially when Sam worked near at hand.

And soon it came about when Marta walked
To get the eggs that Sam went too. They talked
At first about how much crops needed rain,
About the neighbors, and the war in Spain;
Small talk transformed to freely flowing streams
As each shared hidden hopes and secret dreams.
Upon the porch together they would swing
And listen to far-off cicadas sing;
As breezes moved among the spruce tops there,
A scent of lilac filled the evening air.

One quiet night they found a private place
Hidden beneath a willow's swaying grace
And there, watched only by an eye of moon,
His lips met hers with all the warmth of June.
Their fevered vows of separating never,
Echoed their whispered love lasting forever,
Until someone plucks sun and moon from sky
And lakes and rivers wipe their basins dry,
Until the stars snuff out their chandelier
And all the hills and mountains disappear.

When Marta told her parents how she felt,
She thought the hills and rocks and trees would melt;
Her father's face turned several shades of red
And mother nearly toppled over dead.
Said Petra, "Your pronouncement makes me sick;
This farm-hand isn't even Catholic!"
And father added, "None of this will do!
Sam Holland simply isn't right for you;
He knows nothing about our people's ways."
Gray winter shadows darkened Marta's gaze.

Then Father's words thundered and cracked the air,
Despite how Marta cried and tore her hair,
"As swiftly as our cold creek waters flow,
Now just as swiftly Sam must pack and go!"
Standing together in the morning mist
Sam took her face in both his hands and kissed
Her lips and said, "Someday you'll be my wife
And I will find a place to spend our life
Smelling of lilac and chrysanthemum;
I'll write and tell you where and when to come."

Parting with final promises to write,
She wept him down the road, soon out of sight.
Then Marta turned to waiting patiently,
"Was there, perhaps, something today for me?"
She rose excited every single day
Through all of April and through all of May,
Yet into June still nothing had been heard;
July fell silent, not a single word.
An arid August brought September rain,
But Marta never heard from him again.

And who could know her sorrow and her grief
Reflected fluttering in every leaf?
When one day Marta would not leave her room
They brought her brother home to ease her gloom
And Martin told her, "Marta, stop this fuss;
You know that fellow wasn't one of us!"
But on the porch she would no longer swing
Nor listen to far-off cicadas sing
Though breezes moved among the spruce tops there
And scent of lilac filled the evening air.

That year her brother Martin was ordained
Sub-Deacon and then Deacon. There remained
An empty sadness deep in Marta's heart;
Time had not healed what love had torn apart.
She baked the beans, hung wash to dry in air,
And cleaned the cobwebs from the cellar stair.
The next year Martin was ordained a priest
And no one could remember such a feast
For all the neighbors in the countryside
Who basked beneath the glow of Petra's pride.

Assistant Pastor Martin so impressed
His parishes that each thought itself blest,
And when the Bishop heard their accolade,
He called upon his humble priest and made
Him pastor to a parish of some size.
With his own parish, it was no surprise
When Father Martin said that he would need
A good housekeeper; everyone agreed
That Marta was the perfect candidate:
Dependable, resourceful, and sedate.

So Marta followed Martin to each place
He was assigned as pastor. In the space
Of fifty years he preached and sanctified
The souls of thousands. Always by his side
Though seldom seen worked Marta. By and by
His people knew him as Monsignor Sy.
Then one day Marta heard the reverend fall
And found him lifeless, face down in the hall;
She never learned how he had hit his head:
A stroke? Or too much *Johnny Walker Red*?

His eulogy portrayed him as a saint
And sounded somehow out of date and quaint.
Much later Marta found among his things
A little pack of letters tied with strings,
Letters all postmarked fifty years ago,
Unopened still, and clean and white as snow.
Then something caused her sight to swirl and blur:
All of these letters were addressed to her!
Her fingers trembled opening each one
As each revealed more of the morning sun.

"Marta, my love . . . ."   ". . . a perfect place for us . . . ."
"The lilies bloom . . . ."   "Here's money for the bus . . . ."
"I miss you so much . . . ."   "Mountain tops are white . . . ."
"I love you still . . . ."   "Why do you never write?"
Though Marta sometimes dreamed that she would go,
What really would she say or need to know?
Alone upon the porch Marta would swing
And listen to far-off cicadas sing;
As breezes moved among the spruce tops there,
A scent of lilac filled the evening air.

Part Two: The Wedding Dress

"Sold for five dollars!" and the auctioneer
Hammered his gavel down for all to hear.
Five women's hats fashioned so out of style
Even the winning bidder had to smile
Lay neatly on the table in a row
Above the bidding faces down below.
The crowd had stood waiting all afternoon
This breezeless Saturday in early June
To see these household items auctioned off;
They came like cattle to a water trough.

Whatever drove him through the scorching sun
That searing summer? What yarn had time spun
To yank him westward toward a better life
Without employment and without a wife?
He had cranberried in Wisconsin bogs
And trimmed the limbs from Minnesota logs,
Yet when he cut through tall Nebraska corn
With boots cracked, dusty, leather thin and torn,
He never slowed his unrelenting pace
To find somewhere that perfect settling place.

*"And now what have we here? A wedding dress
Worn years ago, adorned without excess. . . ."*
*He held the dress so all could clearly see
It antedated present memory.
A wave of laughter lightly washed the crowd
As many smiles expressed themselves out loud
And sprang from jibes which foster nervous kidding.*
"All right," he said, "and who will start the bidding?"
"Two dollars!" quickly piped up from the rear,
A fragile, paper voice, but crystal clear.

How many miles? How many hills and turns?
How many nights bedded among green ferns?
What hope pulled him along that weary road?
What peaceful dreams lightened his heavy load?
And then one morning, over one more hill
He saw something which made him stop dead still:
A field of lilies stretched beyond his sight
As if snow covered, nearly blinding white,
A soft mist lined the mountain's capping snow,
And warm sun cleared the valley fog below.

*And everyone twisted around to see
Who'd placed this bid with such authority.
A tiny white-haired woman no one knew
Wearing a little hat and dress of blue
Stood all alone and faced this staring crowd,
Lips set determined, confident and proud.
So no one dared to place a higher bid,
As if she'd closed the box and locked the lid.
The auctioneer chanted his monody,
"Two dollars bid – two bid! Do I hear three?"*

Though jobs might melt away like snow, a good
Hard working farm hand always could find food,
And he worked hard. Twilight shadows grew long
And sang to him a dark cicada's song.
He planted purple lilac by his door
But lilac only darkened his life more.
He married Jean to mend the tattered lace
Of memory and fill his hollow space,
But in childbirth she and the baby died.
He buried both beneath his green hillside.

*The crowd in stupefied bewilderment
Could only wonder as to her intent:
Two dollars for a yellowed wedding dress –
What did it mean to her? No one could guess.
And few assembled could remember such
A silence palpable enough to touch.
As one they turned back toward the auctioneer
Who sensed the end of bidding drawing near.
His words jabbed disappointment at the price,
"Two dollars going once – two dollars twice –"*

And after that, though friendly, he withdrew
Into himself and no one ever knew
Why he would sit and listen to the breeze
Among his lilac and his willow trees,
So he grew old as he preferred, alone,
Within a private garden all his own.
One day he fell and had to take to bed
And word on wings among his neighbors spread
Concern and prayers for him, and dark dismay,
But he turned worse and one night passed away.

"Sold for two dollars!" with his gavel's whack,
"Sold to the little lady in the back,"
In sing-song shout so surely she could hear.
And once again the crowd turned toward the rear
To stare this ancient woman down the aisle,
Expressionless, without a hint of smile.
She paid two crumpled dollars for her prize
Then gently took the dress, lowered her eyes,
And slowly stepped the way back she had come
Past looks perplexed, mouths open-jawed and dumb.

Next day at Maggie's Coffee Cup the crowd
Which gathered daily sipped its thoughts out loud:
"Where was that woman from?" "What was her name?"
"I heard that she knew Sam before he came
Out here," Maggie replied during refills,
"Back east somewhere – among Wisconsin's hills."
That day a warm wind swept the marble face
Which marked Sam Holland's final resting place;
Another warmth spread too: someone unknown
Had planted purple lilac by his stone.

Blackwing Requiem

A black cacophony of crows disturbed
Our morning walk; their rowdy, diving wings
Swooped in and out above the line of oaks

Along the ridge dividing Olson's corn
From the neglected graveyard. Suddenly
A hawk burst from the leaves, tumbling into

The corn, its tightly taloned prey struggling
For life. Then somehow freed, the crow sprang back
Into the sanctuary of the trees,

The persevering hawk pursuing close,
Both lost to sight.
                Later on our return,
Walking among the cemetery stones

And noticing how wind and rain and snow
Had smoothed them to illegibility,
Forgotten faces with forgotten names,

We chanced upon a random swirl of black
Dismembered feathers, all that now remained
Of what not long ago had flashed in flight.

Somehow that hungry hawk could sense this place
As one appropriate to shrine this death
And me as one to sing this requiem.

The Onion

I peeled each verbal petal back
    Beyond the one before,
Unfolding insignificance
    To probe truth at its core.

But when that final blossom bent,
    What lay beneath my knife?
Nothing. No truth. No clarity.
    Just one harsh whiff of life.

The Night The Lightning Struck

                                        and killed the cow,
we all sat shuttered up against the storm
and safely cellared, so how could we know
when that white shaft shot through the dark and cracked
that it zapped Moll?
                    Much later in the mist
of morning light we stumbled from our tomb
and saw her lying in the yard, the flies
already in her eyes and crawling in
and out her nostrils.
                    Then Pa dug the hole
down by the creek, came back and looped a rope
around her head and to the Ford, and dragged
Moll's roasted carcass slowly through the long
wet grass.
           I still remember wondering
for what cow-blasphemy God struck her dead.

The Christmas Swallow

That year no elder could remember
A warmer waning of November;
October leaves raked long ago
    Advanced no snow.

About the barnyard swallows whirled,
So magically they swooped and swirled;
Their looping, acrobatic flight
    Filled evening light

And flooded all with melody,
A soft, staccato ecstasy,
Such silver song as never heard
    From throat of bird.

But soon skies filled with fixed formations
All aimed toward southern destinations,
Geese honking arrows shot from bows
    Before the snows.

December saw that sneaking snow
And swallows twittered, "We must go
Before the northwind's stabbing knives
    Take all our lives."

One little swallow turned to tell
The other animals farewell,
"Friends, we'll return to swoop and sing
   In early spring."

"Stay, little swallow," urged the cow,
"As long as weather will allow;
My mooing sounds so dull and wrong,
   Unlike your song."

"Stay, little swallow," pig expressed,
"Stay perched within your cozy nest;
My grunting sounds so crude and wrong,
   Unlike your song."

Swallow replied, "Friends, huddle near;
If we delay and linger here
The frigid northwind's stabbing knives
   Will take our lives."

"Stay, little swallow," clucked the hen,
"Just until snowflakes fall again;
My cackling sounds so harsh and wrong,
   Unlike your song."

"Stay, little swallow," squawked the duck,
"Your music leaves us wonderstruck;
My quacking sounds so coarse and wrong,
    Unlike your song."

"Well, just one day," the swallow said,
"You others wing your way ahead;
Tomorrow we shall rendezvous
    In asters blue."

About the yard the swallow whirled,
So magically it swooped and swirled;
Its looping, acrobatic flight
    Filled evening light

And flooded all with melody,
A soft, staccato ecstasy,
Such silver song as never heard
    From throat of bird.

Next day as swallow readied flight,
The animals begged, "One more night,
Dear swallow, leave us with your cheer:
    Sing for us here."

"Just one more night," the swallow said,
"My other friends have flown ahead
And I must meet my comrades soon,
    By crescent moon."

That one more night turned one more day
And soon two weeks had blown away;
Now swallow knew he'd have to go
    Through swords of snow.

But still they would not let him leave,
"Tonight," they said, "marks Christmas Eve!
We kneel at midnight by our stalls
    Within these walls!"

"We kneel to meet our Savior's birth,
The Lord of heaven and of earth;
Stay with us, swallow, with your song.
    It won't take long."

And so at midnight swallow whirled,
So magically it swooped and swirled;
Its looping, acrobatic flight
    Amid strange light

Flooded them all with melody,
A soft, staccato ecstasy,
Such silver song as never heard
    From throat of bird

While all the animals knelt down
Beneath swallow's melodic crown
Offered for all before this King
    On darting wing.

Next morning, crystal cold and bright,
The swallow lifted into flight,
But as it rose, its farewell note
    Froze in its throat.

It fluttered gracelessly to ground
With no fanfare and with no sound
And no one guessed what beauty died
    That Christmas-tide.

   *   *   *   *

At Christmas noon the heavenly host
With Father and with Holy Ghost
Gathered to hear the Father's voice
    And to rejoice.

"Know that my Son has gone to earth,"
He said, "To give man second birth,
His empty throne at my right hand,
    But understand

Whose sacrifice fulfills my Word. . ."
His eyes sought out a little bird.
"Swallow, who sang so lovingly,
    Please, sing for me."

And so at God's hand swallow whirled,
So magically it swooped and swirled;
Its looping, acrobatic flight
    Amid His light

Flooded that host with melody,
A soft, staccato ecstasy,
Such silver song as never heard
    From throat of bird.

Now as that little swallow sings
For one with healing in His wings,
To Him may this plain music raise
    Garlands of praise.

Old Woman Reminiscing

When I was young the boys would stand
    In line to dance with me.
I still can hear that throbbing band
    Play in my memory.

When I was young boys would stop by –
    Red roses they would bring –
But snow will fly in mid-July
    Before my phone will ring.

When I was young the kissing seemed
    As it would last all night,
But time has teeth I never dreamed
    And I have felt their bite.

When I was young I led the dance
    Through fields of purple clover,
And how I hope for one more chance
    Before the dance is over.

Ain't Got Them Blues
(to be sung with a slow, steady rhythm)

Ain't been no slacker
No red-neck cracker
    This bossman's yacker
    Makes midnight blacker
My gal's a stacker
An all night smacker

    Ain't got them low down hang dog
      Heavy duty soul suckin' blues
      Ain't got them blues.

Mornin' ain't sunny
Nose awful runny
    Ain't got no money
    Hole in my gunny
But she's my honey
My honey bunny

    Ain't got them low down hang dog
      Heavy duty soul suckin' blues
      Ain't got them blues.

Depressed after Reading a Series of Bad Poems, I Recall a Great One by James Wright

And wonder if the book that Wright let fall
    Behind a stone still lies in that same place,
    Its pages weathered, eaten into lace
By insects. Does that lovely cricket's call,
Crossing the distance from that maple stand,
    Still darkly echo there? Do ants still climb
    Transparent shadows up that post? Has time
Eroded memory in shifting sand?
These other poems, neither blood nor bone,
    Fall, feigning silver, as tin flaking rust
        Or withered husks of corn in need of rain
From barely beating, hollow hearts of stone,
    Dry lines stuttered from thick tongues caked with dust,
    Dead words no one will ever read again.

In Memoriam: For Six Poets
(Hart Crane, Vachel Lindsay, Sara Teasdale, Sylvia Plath, John Berryman and Anne Sexton)

Poor Hart, we all
Could only guess
How you had roused
Your sailor boy
To violence
Your ego crushed
Beyond the pain
Of beating fists —
Next morning with
Your friends on deck
Your swollen eyes
And broken lips
Stunned them as you
Slipped overboard
(One said it seemed —
Or had she dreamed —
You strongly stroked
Then disappeared).
What loveliness
Within those eyes
The night before
Still filled your sight
In morning light
Their liquid dark
And beautiful
Pulling toward depths
Wherein you fell
To meet them in
That surging swell
Of sucking sea?

Vachel, your rage
Had set the stage
The year before
No one had asked
You for a song
For such a long
Time silence reigned
Where once your crowd
Had thundered loud
With clapping hands
And stomping feet
In rhythm to
Your poetry
But now no more
Yet worse than your
So fickle fans
It seemed to you
Your muse had fled
From out your head
No music sang
No pipes nor drums
Boomed anymore
Providing spark
Rekindling flames –
What made you think
The fluid fire
Within that jar –
The amber one
Upon the shelf –
Would loose your tongue?

Then Sara's turn
Late Vachel's dear
A regal pair
Of opposites
The wild prince he
Tame princess she
(Once he had swiped
A drop of rain
From off your nose
Placed it within
An envelope
And mailed it to
His home address)
As your hot bath
Loosened those knots
Of loneliness
And weary woe
After the pills
(One–two–three–four
How many more?)
Had induced sleep
Soundlessly deep
For no one's sake
Would you awake
As steam arose
And water leaked
Into your lungs
Leaving no room
For inhaled breath
Just silent death.

Sweet Sylvia
So far from home
And now alone
Amid this rain
This awful gray
And everyday
This dreary fog
On swift impulse
Or careful plan
The children were
Provided for
Their breakfast neat
Beside their beds
Window ajar
Door closed and taped
And then you turned
Your eye to that
Most matronly
Of Death's engines –
Your kitchen stove
And knelt before
Your oven door
Letting its dark
And cozy warmth
Of honey thick
Sweet smelling gas
Drift you toward peace
Forgetfulness
Soft soothing sleep
And lulling dreams.

Then bearded John
Our man of booze
Went for a walk
That winter day
Along the bridge
Somehow you had
Decided that
The time had come
To meet Henry
Your mythic twin
Here face to face
And to embrace
Reality
All you could see
Swirled in a glass
Of crackling ice
Far down below
Sepulchral snow
Invited you
So up you climbed
Over the rail
Waving "Ta-ta!"
To passers-by
And jumped. I'll bet
That if we could
Have listened in
On the way down
We would have heard
You whispering
"Henry!...Henry!"

Anne's time so soon
Your bio held
A history
Of botched attempts
And therapy
A file the size
Of *War and Peace*
And all public
Confessional
Upon the page
Your life a blur
You dressed in fur
Got in your car
And turned the key
The engine sprang
To gaseous life
Then you turned on
The radio
And set the dial
Waiting a while
To file your nails
Perhaps some song
Or lovely voice
Caused you to pause
And close your eyes
Distracting you
Just long enough
That you forgot
The door of the
Garage was closed.

We always seem
To need to find
Some rationale
For such dark scenes.
Perhaps their deaths
Lie purposeless,
Lives blown about
Like autumn leaves,
Grim tragedies
Without intent –
Just let them go.
All we can know
For sure and say:
Death either way
Silenced their song.

A Lullaby For Ean

May honeysuckle match your cheek
    And lilac line your walk;
May music change the words you speak
    To rainbows as you talk.

May pine boughs cradle you at night
    And starlight guide your way;
May wonder lead you into light
    And sunshine fill your day.

May dreams rock you as in a boat
    And sail through every storm,
And may love like an overcoat
    Protect and keep you warm.

A Wedding Blessing
    (for Mary and Steve)

May joy lead you along a path
    Where laughing breezes blow,
And may contentment, like a quilt,
    Warm you in winter snow.

May lilac lighten heavy loads
    And honey sweeten strife,
And may you always find it full,
    This cookie jar of life.

May gentle rains nourish your dreams
    To flowering endeavor,
And may this river we call love
    Flow through your lives forever.

A Memorial

(to my infant sisters who died in a fire which destroyed our home, April 12, 1949, and to my father who died attempting to rescue them)

Death tapped upon my sisters' door
   And whispered, "Time to go."
They woke and dressed and let him in;
   So young, they could not know.

My father heard, tried to object,
   "Then let me take their place!"
Death smiled, "You're also on my list,"
   And touched my father's face.

And we could only stand and watch
   Their flaring, swirling flight,
Until Death's incense stung our eyes
   And hid them from our sight.

Echoes of Ancient Music

Prologue: To Set The Scene . . .

Leda, in Greek mythology, was raped by Zeus who came to her in the form of a swan – and from this union was born Helen of Troy, who was abducted by Paris, one of the Princes of Troy, as his reward for choosing the most beautiful from among the goddesses, Hera, Athena and Aphrodite. Paris, known to the gods for his beauty, intelligence and honesty in judgment, was selected by Zeus to choose from among the three following an incident caused by Eris (goddess of discord) who, as an uninvited guest, threw an apple into a wedding feast bearing the inscription "to the most beautiful." Each of the three goddesses tried to bribe Paris: Hera, by giving him power; Athena, by giving him wisdom; and Aphrodite, by giving him the love of the most beautiful woman in the world. Paris chose Aphrodite and subsequently received Helen. From that act sprang all of the ensuing strife, bloodshed, and death.

Following ten long years of war upon the plains of Troy, Odysseus set sail for his home in Ithaca. That journey home took another ten years, during which he experienced an unbelievable range of difficulties, tasks and adventures. Finally, Odysseus reached Ithaca, only to find his home and his wife besieged by suitors seeking her hand in his absence. Eventually he vanquished them all and reclaimed his proper place in his home and in his homeland.

This sonnet sequence highlights subjective impressions of certain portions of Homer's *The Iliad* and *The Odyssey*. Details relating to Homer's person and life have been lost to history, but his poems still delight readers after three thousand years.

Part One: Revisiting the Walls of Troy

Leda

What special feature drew me to his sight?
Did he see some rare beauty in my face?
My eyes? My mouth? My willow waist? Some grace
About my slender ankles, lean and light?
Now I must tell my husband what occurred,
But will he say I bear some brutish thing?
What if I bear a queen? What if a king?
Will he forgive me? Will he find no word?
I do know this: one day deep in our wood
Strong wings swooped down upon me from afar
And as he slowly feathered through my thighs
My fingers held him, while within his eyes
I saw ten thousand flags unfurl for war
And all our universe awash with blood.

Paris

To choose one out of three, what would you do
If some fair goddess spoke and offered you
Undreamed of power – just grant her request?
I doubt if you would laugh and say, "You jest!"
Or if a second, somewhat fairer, came
To seek your favor, calling you by name,
And offered boundless wisdom – would you say,
"No thanks!" and, smiling, simply walk away?
What if a third one promised you for life
The love of earth's most beautiful as wife,
While she let fall her silken robe to earth,
And stood resplendent there, garbed as in birth?
My finger faltered not and chose the third,
Her gifts more eloquent than any word.

Priam

How hot the passions and the rage of youth!
Why can they not sit quietly at ease
Here underneath our scented laurel trees
In thought, pursuing harmony and truth?
Or if not that, then why not casually
Relax at night before a gentle fire
Composing soothing songs upon the lyre
Or rhapsodizing love in poetry?
Now, since my son has brought that woman here
From Sparta of all places, all my dreams
Fill up with stinking pyres, smoking and red;
At night I wake with horrors in my ear:
Our walls reverberant with wailing screams,
And my sweet, lovely children lying dead.

Helen

How did I cause it? What would you have done
If everyone who chanced to look at you
As you passed by them on some busy street
And caught your eye, would quickly turn away?
My husband always thought me on display,
His trophy, though our light bore little heat,
His smiling consort in the public view.
I knew that I would never bear his son.
But then another came and carried me
Beyond the billows of the eastern sea.
I only wanted peace within that place
And love beyond the contours of my face.
Instead, I learned love triggers war, and worse:
That beauty brandishes a lifelong curse.

Achilles

Bah! Let them wrestle with their tinkling toys
Of war, for I have lost all taste of it.
Within these confines, all alone, I sit
And watch the hagglings of these little boys.
I came with proffered hand to join the fray
Most willingly in answer to their call,
But now my sword and shield hang on this wall
And I will not participate today.
She brought me every morning fresh delight,
Warm noontime sweetness, and cool evening breeze.
Our monarch knew she made my life complete,
But when he took her, victory took flight
And left his armies beaten to their knees.
So let them die and rot in their defeat!

Hector

This morning, with my armor strapped and laced,
My broadsword lashed and belted to my waist,
I met my wife in silence at our door,
Her eyes downcast, weary with dress of war.
She knew whom I would have to meet today,
But neither one of us knew what to say.
I gently touched her cheek, she kissed my hand,
And then I turned to face him on the sand.
That other one, the cause of this campaign,
Whose looks alone could suck away your breath,
Aroused in us the strength to swallow fear,
And now how many on this shore lie slain,
Forced far too soon to feel the sting of death?
Why did my brother have to bring her here?

Odysseus

Penelope! Sweet love, Penelope!
Ten years have lapsed since first I left for war
Upon these plains of Troy and still I see
No end to fighting on this sandy shore.
I wish that I could see our little son,
Telemachus, perhaps along the beach,
Where all of us could laugh and swim and run,
And both of you would lie within my reach.
Wild images upset my sleep last night:
Our warriors packed into a hollow horse
Of wood released, and all of Troy in flames.
What poets ages hence will sing our names,
Once time consumes our deeds within its course
And lifts us into everlasting light?

Part Two: Where Odysseus Sailed

War's End

At sunrise, as the ember kindling dawn
Stretched forth to let her finger-tips ignite
The torch of day, her first phalanx of light
Revealed most of our troops already gone.
A backward glance exposes broken walls
Still smoldering, our victory now clear,
But I intend no further pausing here;
We board our ships, my warriors heed my calls.
Soon masts will bend before the swelling force
Of friendly winds filling our canvas full,
And we will ride the sea beneath our hull
Westward, the anchored stars to guide our course.
Yes, soon we sail this surging, crested foam
Toward Ithaca, toward you, my love, and home.

The Cyclops

So now I tend my sheep as if at night
And yet my careful fingers see them all;
Sometimes on hands and knees I have to crawl
From place to place with only touch for sight.
Considered popular, I once had friends,
But now none ever comes to visit me,
And I am known as one who cannot see;
My all-consuming nightmare never ends.
I view what happened as some dreadful dream,
A grief I try to push beyond my reach.
I rarely go to town; I rarely speak.
Instead I slowly stumble by this stream
Or wander aimlessly down by the beach
To sit alone while salt-spray wets my cheek.

Circe

Just yesterday he came with all his crew
Who lounged around as if they owned the place,
And so I laced their cocktails with a trace
Of something I concoct, my special brew.
They laughed and asked if I would ride my broom,
But when they ate my cheese and sipped my wine,
I had them grunting like a herd of swine,
Cavorting hogs, bumbling from room to room.
On him my magic did not work as planned;
Instead he cast his captive spell on me:
The strange, hypnotic strength within his eyes
Caught all my charms and powers by surprise,
And I fell victim to his recipe,
Transformed to pliant dough beneath his hand.

In the Land of the Dead

At last our ship was swallowed up by night
Within a sea of black, devoid of light,
Where total darkness sucked eye sockets dry,
And we could not distinguish sea from sky.
Sharp, horrid stenches seemed to hang in air
As oozing sulfurs slithered everywhere,
And soon these shadows filled with wailing sighs,
Wild, howling screams, and woeful, sobbing cries.
Such terrors caused us to hallucinate:
We saw and spoke with heroes long since dead
Who warned us of catastrophes to come.
All night we sat in silence, insensate,
Our hands and feet immobile, filled with lead,
Our eyes straining for light, our tongues struck dumb.

The Sirens

Come, let my music, borne upon the wind,
Lull you to sleep at final end of day,
For I can sing your weariness away
And lift all heavy burdens from your mind.
Come, let my music, woven of the sea,
Embroider your distressed and tattered seams,
For I can sing your worries into dreams
And wash anxiety from memory.
Come, let my music, glistening with lights,
Exhume your sorrow from its dark abyss,
For I can sing your sadness into bliss
And rain your tears dry from celestial heights.
Come, let our music fill your ears and eyes
With diamond starbursts blown from evening skies.

Calypso

You must admit you spend your nights with me
In more than just a casual display
Of passing fondness. Then you spend all day
In silent grief, just staring out to sea.
At some point you will surely have to choose
Which course to steer, with each path charting such
Extreme divergence: on the one hand much
To gain, but on the other, much to lose.
Her fragile feelings mimic mortal lace:
Warmth for today, perhaps tomorrow ice,
A love with limits and no guarantee.
I offer an unending, warm embrace,
A daily dash of sparkling dawn as spice,
Eternal love, and immortality.

Penelope

Odysseus, I had not planned to wait
For you for twenty years without one word
From anyone about you. I have heard
Not one small syllable as to your fate.
As for myself, I sit before my loom,
Alone, far from this awful, pressing crowd
And weave, day after day, this ghostly shroud,
Hoping each day to see my husband home.
And now these crows collect in lurid flight
About our eaves; I wish they would depart,
But their raw dissonance lasts all day long.
Tomorrow may my absent sailor's song
Replace the silent shadows in my heart
With melody and harmony and light.

When Death Shall Have Dominion

That day when colors fade to gray
    And eyesight blurs to black,
When lungs' loose gasping leaks away
    And rigid limbs lie slack,

When heartbeat's booming drum has ceased,
    What swallowed song unsung
Will silence, that devouring beast,
    Suck from my knotting tongue?

Love Song

Someday they'll place me in a bed
    Of burnished brass and steel,
A satin pillow at my head
    And ruffles to my heel.

As family and friends file by,
    I hope no one will weep;
With no more than a gentle sigh,
    Imagine me asleep.

Forgive me if I do not nod
    Or greet you if you speak;
I may be occupied with God,
    Refuting His critique.

One thing I ask: that next to me
    You'll rent adjoining space
Where, once time weaves its tapestry,
    Our love will interlace

Like twining dry leaves roused by breeze
    Some autumn afternoon
Blown far above the tallest trees,
    Beyond both sun and moon.

Wind Riders

If you row from the dock at noon
    And I at half past three,
I hope that when you beach your boat
    You'll turn to wait for me.

And if I push off after one
    While you stay until four,
I'll wave and guide you through the mist
    And greet you on the shore.

We'll laugh until tears fill our eyes
    As time and space rescind,
Then, holding one another close,
    We'll ride upon the wind.